C000138950

Raymond Chapman is Emeritus Professor of English in the University of London and a non-stipendiary priest in the Diocese of Southwark. He is a Vice-Chairman of the Prayer Book Society and is the author of numerous literary and religious titles including *Leading Intercessions*, *Rhythms of Prayer* and *Stations of the Resurrection*.

A Pastoral Prayer Book

*Prayers and readings for times of change,
concern and celebration*

Raymond Chapman

CANTERBURY
PRESS

Norwich

© in this compilation Raymond Chapman 1998

First published in 1998 by The Canterbury Press Norwich
(a publishing imprint of Hymns Ancient & Modern Limited
a registered charity)
St Mary's Works, St Mary's Plain
Norwich, Norfolk, NR3 3BH

All rights reserved. No part of this publication which is
copyright may be reproduced, stored in a retrieval
system, or transmitted, in any form or by any means,
electronic, mechanical, photocopying, recording, or
otherwise, without the prior permission of the publisher.

Raymond Chapman has asserted his right under the
Copyright, Designs and Patents Act, 1988, to be identified
as Author of this work

A catalogue record for this book is available
from the British Library

ISBN 1-85311-220-8

Typeset by Rowland Phototypesetting,
Bury St Edmunds, Suffolk
Printed in Great Britain by
Biddles Ltd, Guildford and King's Lynn

Contents

Suggestions for Use

The book offers resource material for pastoral care and support in some of the major joys and sorrows of life. On occasions like baptism and marriage, it may be used as preparation for the more formal and public action of the Church. At times of more private concern, such as moving house or starting a new job, the event itself will be the focus of concern.

Clergy and lay pastoral visitors may find some suggestions to aid their ministry and supplement their own response to the needs of those in their care. Many who are not in any official pastoral capacity will want to be close to their family and friends at special times, to share grief and happiness and to offer prayerful support. No formal commissioning is required to hold an act of worship in a domestic setting, and sometimes those who come simply as people known and trusted may be the most supportive.

No 'leader' is essential; people brought together by a common concern can help one another in readings and prayers. Individuals separated by distance from the situation, or feeling it is not one they should personally enter, can find here material for their intercessions. The person who is alone at a difficult time can perhaps find help in focusing private prayer.

It should be emphasized that each section is not intended as a full 'service' to be followed through from beginning to end in every detail. A short act of worship could certainly take this order if desired, but many will want to select what seems more useful and of course to supplement it as they may themselves be guided.

Each section contains the following:

- A paragraph to introduce the theme and set it in a prayerful context.

- Short passages from both Testaments of the Bible.

- Passages from other sources to aid further reflection.

- Prayers for the occasion.

- A short section of 'dialogue' prayer, marked by the traditional *V* and *R* (versicle and response) which can be divided between the pastoral visitor and the others present, or in any way convenient.

- A passage of meditation, to be shared or used individually at a separate time.

2

Suggestions for Use

- A sentence from Scripture or other sources, to conclude the act of worship and to be taken away for support in recollection.

All material not ascribed to another source is original. Biblical and other extracts have sometimes been compressed, but not otherwise altered. The usage of other writers with regard to personal pronouns, capital letters and gender words has been preserved. Biblical passages, unless otherwise noted, are from the New Revised Standard Version.

The Pastoral Office for All

A pastor is a shepherd, the great biblical image of loving care even at personal cost. It is most wonderfully expressed in the words of Jesus, who called himself the Good Shepherd (John 10:11) and used the example of the shepherd in one of his most beautiful parables about God's love for all (Luke 15:4–7). The clergy are trained in what is known as *pastoralia*, which includes the care of individuals and families in their charge. Although this still remains one of the most important duties of a Christian priest or minister, it is by no means confined to them. Teams of lay people commissioned to assist in this way are found in most parishes and church groups. But every Christian should be a pastor when the need arises. The support of shared praying and consolation has been characteristic of believers from New Testament times. When Peter was imprisoned, his friends gathered to pray for him (Acts 12:5, 12) and James exhorts Christians to support one another in prayer (James 5:16). Like so many things in Christian practice, it is a natural instinct, in this instance that of

4

helping and supporting others, which is sanctified in the love of God.

The touch of personal sympathy is needed today more than ever. The tendency of our time is to make us more remote from one another, communicating by electronic means and making fewer personal encounters. While there are many benefits in these new resources, there is a danger that the coming together of people in their shared humanity begins to fall away. This is as important for our mutual happiness as for our support in trouble.

There are many specialists to help in the problems of life. Doctors, psychiatrists, social workers and trained counsellors have their part which no one must deny. Christians know that human strength alone is not enough and that the support of prayer and meditation draws all things together for good in the divine purpose. In our pastoral care, let us support not only those central to the situation but also those who offer their care in their own ways. Above all, the pastor must be faithful in personal prayer, a channel for God's grace to others.

*

Bear one another's burdens, and in this way you will fulfil the law of Christ.

Galatians 6:2

Occasions of Use

Birth of a Child

There are few events in life so full of deep and mixed emotions as the birth of a child. First and above all, there is joy that a new human being has come into the world, a new witness to the continual miracle of God's gift of life. There is relief and thanksgiving for a safe birth, together with concern for this little creature starting on the long road of growth to maturity. Inevitably, especially with a first child, parents feel some anxiety about the great responsibility which now lies with them. Radical changes in the family routine can cause tensions, and memories of childhood often return vividly. Christian parents in most church traditions will soon be seeking baptism for the new child, but first all these joys and fears can be gathered up and offered to God, the true Father of young and old alike.

*

It was you who formed my inward parts; you knit me together in my mother's womb. I praise you, for I am fearfully and wonderfully made. Wonderful are your works; that I know very well. My frame was not hidden from you, when I was being made in secret, intricately woven in the depths of the earth. Your eyes beheld my unformed substance. In your book were written all the days that were formed for me, when none of them as yet existed.

Psalm 139:13–16

When a woman is in labour, she has pain, because her hour has come. But when her child is born, she no longer remembers the anguish because of the joy of having brought a human being into the world.

John 16:21

Then little children were being brought to Jesus in order that he might lay his hands on them and pray. The disciples spoke sternly to those who brought them; but Jesus said, 'Let the little children come to me, and do not stop them; for it is to such as these that the kingdom of heaven belongs.' And he laid his hands on them and went on his way.

Matthew 19:13–15

Birth of a Child

Sweet babe, in thy face
Holy image I can trace.
Sweet babe, once like thee,
Thy maker lay and wept for me,

Wept for me, for thee, for all,
When he was an infant small.
Thou his image ever see,
Heavenly face that smiles on thee.

Smiles on thee, on me, on all;
Who became an infant small.
Infant smiles are his own smiles;
Heaven and earth to peace beguiles.

William Blake

He saw the lovely, creamy, cool little ear of the baby, a bit of dark hair rubbed to a bronze floss like bronze-dust. And he waited, for the child to become his, to look at him and answer him. It had a separate being, but it was his own child. His flesh and blood vibrated to it. He caught the baby to his breast with his passionate, clapping laugh. And the infant knew him. As the newly-opened, newly-dawned eyes looked at him he wanted them to perceive him, to recognise him. Then he was verified. The child knew him. A queer contortion of laughter came on its face for him. He caught it to his breast, clapping with a triumphant laugh.

D. H. Lawrence

Father in heaven, we give thanks for the birth of this child, your gracious gift to us. Fill us with reverence before the mystery of human life, so that we may praise you as the giver of all good things, and always keep in our hearts the joy of this day.

Grant to this child health of body, mind and spirit. Defend him/her from all dangers and temptations in the years of growing, so that he/she may come to fullness of faith, to serve you in this world and to enter at last into eternal life.

Bless the parents of this child with love, patience and wisdom. Bring their families and friends close to them at this time, to share in the happiness of this birth and to support them in their new way of life. As your Son Jesus knew the love and care of a human home, give to their home the grace that blessed Mary and Joseph in Nazareth.

V   I will be your father, and you will be my sons and daughters,
R   **Says the Lord Almighty.**
V   Children are indeed a heritage from the Lord.
R   **The fruit of the womb a reward.**
V   You shall rejoice before the Lord your God,
R   **You together with your sons and daughters.**

Birth of a Child

V   Your wife will be like a fruitful vine within
     your house.
**R   Your children will be like olive shoots
     around your table.**

Birth is a mystery,
as strong as the mystery of death,
and all life moves between these two
    certainties.

The Bible tells of many births, joyful births,
    sorrowful births,
late births fulfilling promise after hopes had
    failed,
and the miraculous birth that saved our race.

But every birth is a miracle of grace and love,
and we praise them in this dear child,
a new life brought into time and space,
inheritor of all the ages, partaker of glory.

Saints and angels rejoice at this new gift,
this new being to receive the love of God,
enfolded in our prayer and our love.

*

May you see your children's children.
Peace be upon Israel!

Infant Baptism

Our Lord left a command for two acts of obedience to be performed by all who would believe in him and seek to follow him. One was to receive holy communion, and the other was first to come into the Church through baptism. These are the two sacraments which ever since have been celebrated by all the Christian churches. Parents and relations rejoice and are thankful for the birth of a child. Christian parents will bring the new child for baptism, to be received into the great Christian family. We all come into an imperfect world, our natures flawed by the tendency to do wrong which has tainted the human race. Baptism brings us back into a right relationship with God, and although after baptism we may still fall into sin, the way has been opened for us to repent and return, to receive pardon and new strength. The water of baptism is a sign of our spiritual cleansing. It is the death of the old nature and the birth of the new; passing from death to life is more clearly represented in the total immersion which was the practice of the early

Infant Baptism

Church and is still that of some churches today. Parents and godparents must sincerely make solemn promises on behalf of the child who is as yet unable to make a decision.

*

The Lord is my shepherd, I shall not want.
He makes me lie down in green pastures;
he leads me beside still waters;
   he restores my soul.
He leads me in right paths
   for his name's sake.

Psalm 23:1–3

Then Jesus came from Galilee to John at the Jordan, to be baptized by him. John would have prevented him, saying, 'I need to be baptized by you, and do you come to me?' But Jesus answered him, 'Let it be so now; for it is proper for us in this way to fulfil all righteousness.' Then he consented. And when Jesus had been baptized, just as he came up from the water, suddenly the heavens were opened to him and he saw the Spirit of God descending like a dove and alighting on him. And a voice from heaven said, 'This is my Son, the Beloved, with whom I am well pleased.'

Matthew 3:13–17

Do you not know that all of us who have been baptized into Christ Jesus were baptized into his death? Therefore we have been buried with him by baptism into death, so that, just as Christ was raised from the dead by the glory of the Father, so we too might walk in newness of life.

Romans 6:3–4

Dear be the Church that, watching o'er the
 needs
Of infancy, provides a timely shower
Whose virtue changes to a Christian flower
A growth from sinful Nature's bed of weeds!
Fitliest beneath the sacred roof proceeds
The ministration; while parental love
Looks on, and Grace descendeth from above
As the high service pledges now, now pleads.

William Wordsworth

Once in His Name who made thee,
Once in His Name who died for thee,
Once in His Name who lives to aid thee,
We plunge thee in Love's boundless sea.

'Christian', dear child, we call thee;
Threefold the Bath. The name is One:
Henceforth no evil dreams befall thee,
Now is thy Heavenly rest begun.

John Keble

Infant Baptism

The Church is Catholic, universal; so are all her actions. All that she does belongs to all. When she baptises a child, that action concerns me, for that child is thereby connected to that Head which is my Head too, and engrafted into that body whereof I am a member.

John Donne

★

God our Father, we give thanks for this child whom we are now about to bring to baptism. Grant that this life, begun in the body, may be renewed in the spirit. May your love guide and protect him/her day by day and year by year; may he/she grow into the faith which is to be professed on his/her behalf.

We pray that as our human family is enriched by this new member, the love that we have for one another may be strengthened by our fellowship in the family of all Christian people which N is now to enter.

Dear Lord, give grace to the parents and godparents of this child, so that they may be true to their promises, nurturing the faith of N by their prayers and example. Grant that their own faith shall be confirmed and increased by the duty which they now accept, so that all may grow together towards greater fullness of life.

We dedicate this child to the service of Jesus Christ,
following his example and obeying his command.
May the Church of God bless this new member and
be blessed in him/her.

> *V* You will receive the gift of the Holy Spirit,
> ***R* For the promise is for you, and for your
>   children.**
> *V* There is one body and one Spirit,
> ***R* One Lord, one faith, one baptism.**
> *V* Go and make disciples of all nations,
> ***R* Baptizing them in the name of the Father
>   and of the Son and of the Holy Spirit.**
> *V* Repent and be baptized in the name of Jesus
>   Christ,
> ***R* So that your sins may be forgiven.**

There is no life without water –
most of our bodies, much of our world, are
    water;
water is life, water is death,
we cannot live in it or without it.

This is the strange water, God's water,
the water that kills and makes alive,
that kills the evil no human will can conquer,
that gives new life to the living.

Infant Baptism

Water is relief in a dry land when thirst is
    raging:
this is the living water,
quenching thirst not in the flesh but in the soul.

Water washes the soiled, the unclean, the
    tainted:
this is the pure water
that washes away the dirt we cannot see.

Water fills all that it enters and takes its shape –
pools, lakes, rivers, oceans:
this is the boundless water
that fills the whole person and provides all its
    needs.

In the beginning, the Spirit of God moved on
    the face of the waters.

May he move in power through the water of
    this baptism.

*

Be the eye of God dwelling with you,
The foot of Christ in guidance with you,
The shower of the Spirit pouring on you,
Richly and generously.

Carmina Gaedelica

Adult Baptism, Confirmation or Admission to Church Membership

Whether one is baptized in infancy or not, the time comes when a personal decision and declaration of Christian faith has to be made. Some churches postpone baptism until the person is old enough to take this step, while others require that the promises made previously in baptism should be confirmed when full church membership begins. In most churches, this is the time of admission to the other Gospel sacrament, the Holy Communion. It is a joyful and solemn moment in the Christian life, to be prepared for with instruction in the faith and personal prayer. If one has been baptized as an infant, it is good to read the service then performed and take responsibility for the promises which were made by godparents. This is the time of accepting the full privileges and obligations of the Christian community, a recognition that no one can be a

Baptism, Confirmation or Admission to Church

Christian in isolation for we are members one of another, united in Christ. Those who have gone before in this way will be eager to welcome and nourish the faith newly affirmed.

★

Wash me thoroughly from my iniquity,
   and cleanse me from my sin.
You desire truth in the inward being;
   therefore teach me wisdom in my secret
   heart.
Purge me with hyssop, and I shall be clean;
   wash me, and I shall be whiter than snow.
Create in me a clean heart, O God.
   and put a new and right spirit within me.

Psalm 51:2, 6, 7, 10

I am the vine, you are the branches. Those who abide in me and I in them bear much fruit, because apart from me you can do nothing. Whoever does not abide in me is thrown away like a branch and withers; such branches are gathered, thrown into the fire, and burned. If you abide in me, and my words abide in you, ask for whatever you wish, and it will be done for you. My Father is glorified in this, that you bear much fruit and become my disciples.

John 15:5–8

21

You are a chosen race, a royal priesthood, a holy nation, God's own people, in order that you may proclaim the mighty acts of him who called you out of darkness into his marvellous light.

1 Peter 2:9

God's child in Christ adopted – Christ my all –
What that earth boasts were not lost cheaply, rather
Than forfeit that blest name, by which I call
The Holy One, the Almighty God, my Father?
Father! in Christ we live, and Christ in Thee,
Eternal Thou, and everlasting we.
The heir of heaven, henceforth I fear not death:
In Christ I live! In Christ I draw the breath
Of the true life! Let then earth, sea and sky
Make war against me! On my front I show
Their mighty master's seal! In vain they try
To end my life, that can but end its woe.
Is that a deathbed where a Christian dies?
Yea! but not his: 'tis Death himself that dies.

S. T. Coleridge

After that, by the help of the water of new birth, the stain of former years had been washed away, and a light from above, serene and pure, had been infused into my reconciled heart, after that, by the agency of the Spirit breathed from heaven, a second birth had restored one to a new man; then,

22

in a wonderful manner, doubtful things at once began to assure themselves to me, hidden things to be revealed, dark things to be enlightened.

St Cyprian

The grace, the beautiful gift, which by this means we receive, is declared to be a death unto sin and a new birth unto righteousness: that is to say, the person's true condition is made plain, namely that (to use the startling vigorous language of St Paul) he should be a corpse so far as the influence of sin is concerned, and full of new life and energy with regard to righteousness. The actual fact of Baptism being not only an outward sign, that as water washes the body so God washes the man himself, but is also a means whereby evil is destroyed, and life, conscious personal life, produced.

Stewart Headlam

*

Loving God, be gracious to your servant who desires to enter fully into membership of your Church. We give thanks for your guidance through the years that has brought him/her to this time of decision. As he/she joins the company of Christians, strengthen him/her in faith, to be a witness to the world of your sustaining and redeeming love, and to continue in your service even to the death of the body and the dawn of eternal life.

We pray for those who will receive this new member into their fellowship, that they will welcome him/her and cherish his/her faith so that they may grow in worship together. May they, and all Christian people, be a true family of love, always ready to receive and uphold any who come as strangers and seekers, following the call of God.

> V   In all your ways acknowledge him,
> **R   And he will direct your path.**
> V   I have chosen the way of faithfulness:
> **R   I set your ordinances before me.**
> V   You are my refuge and my fortress,
> **R   My God in whom I trust.**
> V   From his fullness we have all received
> **R   Grace upon grace.**

Life is full of new departures, the rites of
  passage:
some are chosen willingly, others seem to
  happen of themselves,
but all are in the hand of God, part of his
  purpose.

Baptism, Confirmation or Admission to Church

We cannot find the way by ourselves,
we wander and go astray out of the path,
yet each of us must make a personal choice
    when the time comes.

Alone, we are lost sheep, broken branches,
    barren soil;
in Christ we are enfolded, fruitful, fertile,
united in him with all the faithful,
the great company of past, present and to come.

By grace, we come into the Kingdom,
into the fellowship of all the saints,
of prophets and martyrs, heroes of the faith.

Every soul is precious before God,
the ordinary, weak, fallible who come to him
he will never cast out.

*

May you have a full reward from the Lord God of
Israel, under whose wings you have come for refuge.

Engagement

At one time the engagement, or betrothal, was regarded as a formal ceremony leading into the marriage service. It was sometimes performed as a solemn contract at a time before the full marriage took place. The first part of our marriage service is in fact derived from the former betrothal ceremony. Today an engagement is not celebrated so formally, but it is still usually marked by public announcement and the giving of a ring or rings. It is the time when a couple declare that they have found in each other a love greater than ordinary friendship or attraction and are sure that they want to be together for the rest of their lives. It is right that from the start of their engagement until their marriage they should offer their intention to God and seek his guidance in all the plans and preparations that must be made. They will learn to pray together and to understand more and more how their new life is to be lived in faith.

★

Engagement

My beloved speaks and says to me: 'Arise, my love, my fair one, and come away; for now the winter is past, the rain is over and gone. The flowers appear on the earth; the time of singing has come, and the voice of the turtle-dove is heard in our land. The fig tree puts forth its figs, and the vines are in blossom; they give forth fragrance. Arise, my love, my fair one, and come away. Many waters cannot quench love, neither can floods drown it. If one offered for love all the wealth of one's house, it would be utterly scorned.

Song of Solomon 2:10–13, 8:7

Beloved, let us love one another, because love is from God; everyone who loves is born of God and knows God. Whoever does not love does not know God, for God is love. God's love was revealed among us in this way: God sent his only Son into the world so that we might live through him. In this is love, not that we loved God but that he loved us and sent his Son to be the atoning sacrifice for our sins. Beloved, since God loved us so much, we also ought to love one another.

1 John 4:7–11

Let me not to the marriage of true minds
Admit impediments. Love is not love
Which alters when it alteration finds,
Or bends with the remover to remove.
Oh no, it is an ever-fixed mark
That looks on tempests and is never shaken;
It is the star to every wandering bark,
Whose worth's unknown, although his height be
taken.

William Shakespeare

God, who art Three in One,
All things comprehending,
Wise Father, valiant Son,
In the Spirit blending:
Grant us love's eternal three –
Friendship, rapture, constancy;
Lord, till our lives be done,
Grant us love unending,
Bless us, God of loving.

Jan Struther

*

Heavenly Father, bless this couple now drawn together in mutual love: be with them in the time of planning and learning, of new discovery in the new life they are beginning. Support them in their preparation, bring them to the day of their marriage

28

and guide them through their lives in the way that shall be your will for them. Bless also their families and friends who share their joy and will be enriched by love fulfilled.

We give thanks to God for the gift of human love and pray that it may be an image of the divine love: not selfish, not excluding, but drawing others into its radiance, making the world richer by its presence. We ask him to fill this and all loves of men and women with the beauty of holiness, a glimpse in this life of the glory that is to come in life eternal.

V Our help comes from the Lord,
R Who made heaven and earth.
V The steadfast love of the Lord is from
     everlasting to everlasting,
R And his righteousness to children's children.
V Love is patient, love is kind,
R It does not insist on its own way.
V Love bears all things, endures all things:
R Love never ends.

That two can be more than twice one
is one of the oldest truths of human experience.

But it is always new, fresh, unexpected,
declared in words of spring, flowers, sunrise,
    new pastures.

There is no speech that can make it known in
   its fullness,
only the need to give thanks for the joy,
thanks to the other, the beloved,
thanks to those who have brought them
   together, each to each,
thanks above all to God for the wonder of grace.

It is a time for exploring, taking new paths,
but no longer alone, solitary in the seeking.

Now we join the numberless who have followed
   God's way,
men and women together through the ages,
   sharing his guidance.

This is a bright morning, another first day of
   creation:
may its light never grow dim, while life shall
   last.

★

God created humankind in his image, in the image
of God he created them; male and female he
created them.

Wedding

All major religions celebrate marriage with a special ceremony. It is a natural human desire, leading to an act of will that should be sanctified before God. Christian marriage services have adopted some older customs, such as the giving of rings which was part of the ancient Roman cult. Christians take a high view of marriage, which is contracted by the free choice and public declaration of the couple, but is also to be seen within faith as a lifelong commitment to another person. A wedding is in one way a very private occasion, focusing on the union of one man and one woman; but it is also a public occasion, because so many aspects of their relationship with others will be changed. A Christian couple will surely prepare for their wedding day with deep thought and earnest prayer, for as **The Book of Common Prayer** *reminds us, marriage is 'not to be taken in hand unadvisedly, lightly or wantonly'.*

★

God created humankind in his image, in the image of God he created them; male and female he created them. God blessed them, and God said to them, 'Be fruitful and multiply, and fill the earth and subdue it.'

Genesis 1:28–8

Blessed are you, O God of our ancestors,
    and blessed is your name in all generations for
    ever.
Let the heavens and the whole creation bless
    you for ever.
You made Adam, and for him you made his
    wife Eve as a helper and support.
From the two of them the whole human race
    has sprung.
You said, 'It is not good that the man should be
    alone;
    let us make a helper for him like himself.'

Tobit 8:5–6

Jesus said, 'Have you not read that the one who made them at the beginning made them male and female, and said, "For this reason a man shall leave his father and mother and be joined to his wife, and the two shall become one flesh"? So they are no longer two, but one flesh. Therefore

32

Wedding

what God has joined together, let no one separate.'

Matthew 19:4–6

Let endless Peace your steadfast hearts accord,
And blessed Plenty wait upon your board;
And let your bed with pleasures chaste abound,
That fruitful issue may to you afford,
Which may your foes confound,
And may your joys redound
Upon your bridal day, which is not long.

Edmund Spenser

I can conceive no earthly happiness greater than
to be given by God the whole of the earthly, nay,
more than the earthly, the whole of the human
love of another. This is one of God's greatest gifts,
one of the closest symbols of what He is, and of
the union between Himself and us. May you
richly enjoy this great gift, and may it enlarge the
power of your love, and help you to turn with yet
a larger heart to His, and Him.

Bishop Edward King

*

Gracious God, look with favour on this man and
this woman, whose love will soon unite them as
one. Bless the day of their wedding, both with joy in

fulfilment and with sincerity in their lifelong vows. Grant that their love shall grow day by day and year by year, holding them faithful to one another, and obedient to your will for them. May they find mutual strength, trusting in your strength alone to keep them firm until the end.

Loving Father, bless all who will share in the joy of this couple as families, friends or colleagues. May they be enriched by the power of united love, and be ready themselves to give support when it is needed. We pray that this marriage shall abound with love for others and desire for the coming of your Kingdom.

May the Lord with his favour look mercifully upon you, and fill you with all grace, that you may so live together in this life that in the world to come you may have life everlasting.

- V   Your wife will be like a fruitful vine within your house,
- **R   Your children like olive shoots around your table.**
- V   Children are a heritage from the Lord:
- **R   May you see your children's children.**
- V   May the Lord bless you with his mercy,
- **R   May he bring your lives to fulfilment,**
- V   May he grant you all happiness together,
- **R   And may you grow old together.**

Wedding

So many have trodden this path, but it is always
    new:
there is an unknown way to be walked together
because there is no one else like the one who is
    loved.

After all the preparation, the months of
    excitement,
the day itself passes quickly, a dream, a glimpse
    of wonder.

But it is just beginning, and not for two only,
because their love will spread out into the world
like ripples on a still lake, like the radiance of a
    clear light.

There will be a new generation to nurture in
    love and faith,
an older generation to care for patiently as the
    years pass,
people known deeply, or for a little while,
all drawn into a love that is secret and yet open.

Marriage is the figure of a mystical union,
the Church is the Bride of Christ:
we are beginning something bigger than we can
    understand,
trusting to its part in the divine purpose.

*

Blessed are they that fear the Lord and walk in his
ways.

Wedding Anniversary

The wedding anniversary is an occasion for thanksgiving and celebration. Popular custom has given names to special times like the silver and golden wedding, and to others less well known. It is a day when Christians will certainly want to remember the importance to faith of the home and family, celebrated in the Bible and the teaching of the Church. As the couple return thanks for their life together, they will think over what the past year has brought in their relationship with one another and those close to them. Friends who send cards or share their celebration will be asked to pray for their future. Today many couples like to find an occasion for returning to the church where they were married, and there renew their vows. On special anniversaries, they may request a service of thanksgiving there or in the church where they now worship.

*

Happy is the husband of a good wife; the number of his days will be doubled. A loyal wife brings joy to her husband, and he will complete his years in peace. A good wife is a great blessing; she will be granted among the blessings of the man who fears the Lord. Whether rich or poor, his heart is content, and at all times his face is cheerful.

Ecclesiasticus 26:1–4

Husbands should love their wives as they do their own bodies. He who loves his wife loves himself. For no one ever hates his own body, but he nourishes and tenderly cares for it, just as Christ does for the church. For this reason a man will leave his father and mother and be joined to his wife, and the two will become one flesh.

Ephesians 5:28–31

All kings and all their favourites,
All glory of honours, beauties, wits,
The sun itself, which makes times as they pass,
Is elder by a year now than it was
When thou and I first one another saw:
All other things to their destruction draw,
Only our love hath no decay;
This no tomorrow hath, nor yesterday,
Running it never runs from us away,
But truly keeps his first, last, everlasting day.

John Donne

Wedding Anniversary

Those that have loved longest love best. To those who have lived long together, everything heard and everything seen recalls some pleasure communicated, or some benefit conferred, some petty quarrel, or some slight endearment. Esteem of great powers, or amiable qualities newly discovered, may embroider a day or a week, but a friendship of twenty years is interwoven with the texture of life.

Samuel Johnson

*

Gracious God, Father of all, we give thanks for another year of lives shared in human love and in your love that never fails. Bless this couple in all that is yet to come, confirming and strengthening in them the vows which they have made to one another in your name. Keep them faithful until they must part in death and bring them together at last in eternal life.

Bless all who have shared the delight of this married life and been enriched by its mutual love. As they rejoice on this anniversary day, give them grace to continue in support and prayer and to find in this family a sign of the family of all Christian people united in fellowship and love.

A Pastoral Prayer Book

V   Remember the days of old,
R   Consider the years long past.
V   Lord, you have been our dwelling place
R   In all generations.
V   This is the day that the Lord has made:
R   Let us rejoice and be glad in it.
V   Surely goodness and mercy shall follow me
R   All the days of my life.

Another year, and the shared living has grown
    more familiar:
but true love does not fade with familiarity.

The dazzling dawn settles into the
    all-embracing light of day
and the spring bud opens into long summer
    flowering.

Recall now what the vows really meant,
made on a day that seemed like a first day of
    creation.

Perhaps riches have increased or diminished,
perhaps health has been strong or failing:
but the promise was for life and to life's end
so may this day offer a fresh Amen.

Constancy and faithfulness are the attributes of
    God himself
and he gives strength to those who call to him
    for help.

Wedding Anniversary

This is the day to remember, to give thanks for
    all that has been
and trust for all that is to come.

★

God's compassion does not fail, and his mercy is
new every morning.

Separation or Divorce

The separation or divorce of a married couple is one of the most difficult events for Christians to cope with. The Bible generally assumes marriage to be a lifelong commitment, and this is affirmed by the words of Jesus about divorce and remarriage (Mark 10:5–12). Marriage discipline varies in different churches, but none can regard separation or divorce as normative for Christians. Yet the frequency of marriage breakdowns today cannot be ignored, and these situations need as much pastoral care as other crises of life. Separation must arouse many emotions, with sorrow, guilt, anger and anxiety among them. Our feelings and motives are seldom uncomplicated and this crisis focuses uncertainty. It is certainly, like all times of sadness, something to be offered openly to our God of compassion, seeking his help to repent and to forgive. If the couple are not able to pray together, families and friends will want to uphold them in prayer at such a time.

★

Separation or Divorce

As a father has compassion for his children, so the Lord has compassion for those who fear him. For he knows how we were made; he remembers that we are dust. But the steadfast love of the Lord is from everlasting to everlasting on those who fear him, and his righteousness to children's children, to those who keep his covenant, and remember to do his commandments.

Psalm 103:13–14, 17–18

Do not judge, and you will not be judged; do not condemn, and you will not be condemned. Forgive, and you will be forgiven; give, and it will be given to you. Why do you see the speck in your neighbour's eye, but do not notice the log in your own eye? Or how can you say to your neighbour, 'Friend, let me take out the speck in your eye', when you yourself do not see the log in your own eye? You hypocrite, first take the log out of your own eye, and then you will see clearly to take the speck out of your neighbour's eye.

Luke 6:37–8, 41–2

With all my will, but much against my heart,
We two now part.
My very dear,
Our solace is the sad road lies so clear.
It needs no art,
With faint, averted feet,

43

And many a tear,
In our opposed paths to persevere.
Go thou to East, I West.
We will not say
There's any hope, it is so far away.
Perchance we may,
Where now this night is day,
And even through faith of still averted feet,
Making full circle of our banishment,
Amazed meet;
The bitter journey to the bourne so sweet
Seasoning the termless feast of our content
With tears of recognition never dry.

Coventry Patmore

Forgiving love is a possibility only for those who
know that they are not good, who feel themselves
in need of divine mercy, who know that the differ-
ences between the good man and the bad man are
insignificant in God's sight.

Reinhold Niebuhr

Go from me. Yet I feel that I shall stand
Henceforward in thy shadow. Nevermore
Alone upon the threshold of my door
Of individual life, I shall command
The uses of my soul, nor lift my hand
Serenely in the sunshine as before,
Without the sense of that which I forbore,

44

Separation or Divorce

Thy touch upon the palm. The widest land
Doom takes to part us, leaves thy heart in mine
With pulses that beat double. What I do
And what I dream include thee, as the wine
Must taste of its own grapes. And when I sue
God for myself, He hears that name of thine,
And sees within my eyes, the tears of two.

Elizabeth Barrett Browning

*

Loving Father, we come before you in sorrow and uncertainty, knowing that the secrets of every heart are known to you and that your love never fails. Forgive the wrongs and errors that have arisen in this marriage, and grant that all that has been good shall not perish but bear fruit in ways that now are beyond our sight. May the lessons of the past serve to create a better future for both of these, your children.

O God, since your will is that none of your little ones should be lost, bless those who now are going out to take their ways apart from each other. May they know your guiding presence as they follow their own paths, and your healing power in their loneliness. Bless also the families and friends who are touched by their parting, with your comfort in sorrow and your power to uphold and heal.

V   Put away from you all bitterness and wrath
      and anger:
R   Do not fret – it leads only to evil.
V   Do not judge, and you will not be judged,
**R   Do not condemn, and you will not be
      condemned.**
V   Forgive us our trespasses
R   As we forgive those who trespass against us.
V   Forgive one another
R   As God for Christ's sake has forgiven you.

When we seem to walk alone, we are not alone
because we walk with God even in loneliness.

When light turns to darkness, we are not
      helpless,
because Christ, the light of the world, shines on
      us.

When we go into the wilderness we are not lost
because God makes new paths for the
      wandering feet.

He knows our frailty, our imperfection,
and receives us when we come, offering only
      our weakness.

Sorrow and anger and regret, he understands
      them all
and out of them will make all things new.

Separation or Divorce

It is not anger but resentment that devours love,
not repentance but guilt that destroys hope:
if we avoid them, what has been good will not
  perish.

Put your hand into the hand of God,
go forward, lonely but not alone.

*

God has said, 'I will be with you: I will not fail
you or forsake you.'

Birthday

The anniversary of birth is celebrated in various ways throughout the world, in many religions and cultures. It is a day on which to remember that every human life is unique, a precious gift from God and sustained day by day through his love. It is a day to praise him for life itself, for preservation to this time and continued blessings. It is a day to be shared with those who are close to us, to know that we do not live to ourselves alone but that all we do and are must touch many others. A birthday may bring mixed feelings as the years pass, and we begin to look back more readily than forward. Whatever our age or condition, it is a landmark in the journey through life, a day on which to offer again to God our part in his great purpose.

*

O God, from my youth you have taught me, and I still proclaim your wondrous deeds. So even to old age and grey hairs, O God, do not forsake me,

Birthday

until I proclaim your might to all the generations
to come. Your power and your righteousness, O
God, reach the high heavens.

Psalm 71:17–19

I give thanks to my God always for you because
of the grace of God that has been given you in
Christ Jesus. He will also strengthen you to the
end, so that you may be blameless on the day of
our Lord Jesus Christ. God is faithful; by him you
were called into the fellowship of his Son, Jesus
Christ our Lord.

1 Corinthians 1:4, 8–9

Do not worry, saying, 'What will we eat?' or 'What
will we drink?' or 'What will we wear?' For it is
the Gentiles who strive for all these things; and
indeed your heavenly Father knows that you need
all these things. But strive first for the kingdom
of God and his righteousness, and all these things
will be given to you as well.

Matthew 6:31–3

My birthday. I can only record the fact with great
gratitude. The 'tale' of our life is very marvellous.
The teaching that has enabled me, through God's
grace to teach others! How untrue any biography
– even an autobiography – of any human being

49

must be! How much there is which can never be told except to God, but on which all that is really life has depended.

Elizabeth Sewell

When all thy mercies, O my God,
  My rising soul surveys,
Transported with the view I'm lost
  In wonder, love and praise.

Unnumbered comforts to my soul
  Thy tender care bestowed
Before my infant heart conceived
  From whom those comforts flowed.

Through every period of my life
  Thy goodness I'll pursue,
And after death in distant worlds
  The glorious theme renew.

Joseph Addison

*

O God, Father of all, we give thanks for the life which began on this day, and for your love that has preserved and guided it through the years. Forgive all that has gone astray from the right path, grant time and grace for amendment, strengthen and increase all that is good; lead onward through the time that remains in your purpose until this earthly life ends at the beginning of life eternal.

We pray too for all whose lives are linked with the one who is in our hearts today. As we rejoice together, we pray for blessings on family and friends, those who share in work and those whose lives touch this life only briefly. We remember those who were once near and are now separated by distance or death, asking that your grace will unite them again in love, now and for ever.

Almighty and most merciful Father, who hast brought me to the beginning of another year, grant me so to remember thy gifts, and so to acknowledge thy goodness, as that every year and day which thou shalt yet grant me may be employed in the amendment of my life, and in the diligent discharge of such duties as thy Providence shall allot me. Grant me, by thy grace, to know and to do what thou requirest. Give me good desires, and remove those impediments which may hinder them from effect. Forgive me my sins, negligences and ignorances, and when at last thou shalt call me to another life, receive me to everlasting happiness, for the sake of Jesus Christ our Lord.

Samuel Johnson

A Pastoral Prayer Book

V   This is the day that the Lord has made,
R   Let us rejoice and be glad in it.
V   O give thanks to the Lord, for he is good,
R   For his steadfast love endures for ever.
V   Jesus came that we might have life
R   And have it more abundantly.
V   So teach us to number our days
R   That we may apply our hearts unto wisdom.

The day of birth, like the day of death, is not
    ours to command.

This very day, many lives are beginning and
    many ending
while we rejoice in a life that continues,
while we show with cards and gifts and visits
that every life is itself a gift, a present for us all.

Another year, with its regrets and its pleasures
is such a little time before God, so much for us,
and this day is a resting-place, a time of ease,
a time to look back on the reality of the journey
    past,
and to look forward in trust on the journey that
    lies before.

Because life is precious, a daily miracle,
may each day to come be a new birth,
a new claiming the mercy of God the Lifegiver.

★

Birthday

Surely goodness and mercy shall follow me all the days of my life.

New Job

Change is often upsetting, and particularly change which affects such a large area of life as our daily work. Whether it is the first job of a lifetime, a move after many years in one place, or a return to work after caring for a family, there is inevitable anxiety about coming to work with people who already know each other in that situation. A change of job is much more frequent today than in the past and may mean a radical change of location. But although conditions are different, the Bible tells of many calls to new tasks, often resisted at first. Moses, Isaiah and Jeremiah were all alarmed at what they were being asked to do, and felt unequal to it until God assured them that they went not in their own strength but in his. The disciples and St Paul had to leave their old way of life and begin a new one. What most of us have to do every day may seem far from these great happenings, but all work is a vocation if we will make it so and try to discern God's will for us within it.

★

New Job

Do not let loyalty and faithfulness forsake you;
bind them round your neck, write them on the
tablet of your heart. So you will find favour and
good repute in the sight of God and of people.
Trust in the Lord with all your heart, and do not
rely on your own insight. In all your ways
acknowledge him, and he will make straight your
paths. Do not be wise in your own eyes; fear the
Lord, and turn away from evil.

Proverbs 3:3–7

Do not worry about anything, but in everything
by prayer and supplication with thanksgiving let
your requests be made known to God. And the
peace of God, which surpasses all understanding,
will keep your hearts and your minds in Christ
Jesus.

Philippians 4:6–7

As Jesus passed along the Sea of Galilee, he saw
Simon and his brother Andrew casting a net into
the lake – for they were fishermen. And Jesus said
to them, 'Follow me and I will make you fish for
people.' And immediately they left their nets and
followed him.

Mark 1:16–18

Christ has many services to be done; some are easy, others more difficult; some bring honour, others bring reproach; some are suitable to our natural inclinations and temporal interests, others are contrary to both. In some we may please Christ and please ourselves; but there are others in which we cannot please Christ except by denying ourselves. Yet the power to do this is assuredly given us in Christ. We can do all things in him who strengthens us.

Methodist Covenant Service

To make our labour or employment an acceptable service unto God, we must carry it on with the same spirit and temper, that is required in giving of alms, or any work of piety. For if, 'whether we eat or drink, or whatsoever we do', we must 'do all to the glory of God'; if 'we are to use this world as if we used it not'; if we are to 'present our bodies a living sacrifice, holy, acceptable to God;' if 'we are to live in faith and not by sight', and to 'have our conversation in heaven'; then it is necessary that the common way of our life, in every state, be made to glorify God by such tempers as make our prayers and adorations acceptable to Him.

William Law

New Job

If on our daily course our mind
Be set to hallow all we find,
New treasures still of countless price
God will provide for sacrifice.

The trivial round, the common task
Will furnish all we need to ask:
Room to deny ourselves, a road
To bring us daily nearer God.

John Keble

There must be a beginning of any great matter, but
the continuing unto the end until it be thoroughly
finished yields the true glory.

Francis Drake

*

Dear God, thank you for the opportunity of this new
work. Grant a good beginning and a faithful continuing for as long as it shall last. Guide and direct the
tasks of each day, with light to perceive your will,
strength to perform it and grace to accept it willingly
for your sake.

We pray for all who will be affected by this change
of work; for family and friends who will hear of new
names and new activities; and to all those with
whom the work will be shared, give grace to make

good relationships and to be patient with those who may be difficult and insecure. May there be blessings for many people in this new enterprise.

V   In all your ways acknowledge him
R   And he will make straight your paths.
V   People go out to their work
R   And to their labour until the evening.
V   Everyone's work will be made manifest,
R   For the day will declare it.
V   Come to me, all you that are weary and
       carrying heavy burdens
R   And I will give you rest.

When people say, 'I have done no work this
    week for God,'
they usually think of collecting for missions,
    sick visiting,
arranging flowers in the church: and these are
    good works.

But all work is work for God if we wish it to be
    so,
if it is an offering of ability matched with
    opportunity –
and neither may seem very remarkable to
    ourselves or others.

**Work is for and with other people, God's people,
sometimes happily as if in a fertile valley,**

New Job

sometimes like a wilderness at the heart of a
    populous city
where it is hard to discern the will and the
    purpose.

The living water springs out of the wilderness,
the honest offering of self is always accepted
and the seed grows secretly, day by day.

*

Whatever your hand finds to do, do with your
might.

Moving House

Moving to a new house was not always so common an experience as it is today. Many people were born, lived and died in the same home, and a move was often the result of some unexpected good or bad fortune. In our modern society we are likely to move several times in our lives, perhaps for new employment, opportunities for children or retirement. It is quite a stressful time, for the change from familiar circumstances is accompanied by considerable legal and social demands. Feelings may be of both sadness and excitement or one of these may be dominant. Whatever the circumstances, it is an occasion which, like all significant moments in life, the Christian should commit to God for sustaining and guidance. In faith, we can look forward positively to the new opportunities and the new people we shall meet. Above all, it is a time to remember that God is not limited to any location or any condition of life.

*

Moving House

You who live in the shelter of the Most High,
  who abide in the shadow of the Almighty,
Will say to the Lord, 'My refuge and my fortress;
  My God, in whom I trust.'
Because you have made the Lord your refuge,
  the Most High your dwelling-place
no evil shall befall you,
  no scourge come near your dwelling.

Psalm 91:1–2, 9–10

Come now, you who say. 'Today or tomorrow we will go to such and such a town and spend a year there, doing business and making money.' Yet you do not even know what tomorrow will bring. What is your life? For you are a mist that appears for a little while and then vanishes. Instead you ought to say, 'If the Lord wishes, we will live and do this or that.'

James 4:13–15

I can quite understand how you must feel the breaking up of the old home. After all, in spite of position, honour, money, there is something in the memory of home which speaks of a higher pleasure than those things can give us. It tells us, I think, of the true joy in the eternal home, to which, I trust, we are one by one being taken. The world certainly is not satisfying, and must always be full of trouble, and division, and confusion. We must do our best in it, and with it, but our real life, and rest, and satisfaction is not to be looked for here, but above.

Bishop Edward King

★

Merciful Father, bless those who are now going to a new home. Be close to them in all that must be done, leading them as a tender shepherd to fresh pastures. Strengthen them to meet change with confidence in your love that never changes. Give them grace to make new friends and to bring blessings to those among whom they are soon to live.

We rejoice in all that has been good and pleasant in this house. May we leave it in peace and calm, thankful for what is past and trusting for what is to come. We pray that those who come to live here shall be blessed in all they do and find it a strong place of comfort, rest and love.

V Here we have no lasting city:
R We are looking for the city which is to come.
V Peace be within your walls
R And security within your towers.
V My people will abide in a peaceful habitation,
R In secure dwellings, and in quiet resting-places.

Moving House

V In all your ways acknowledge him
R And he will make straight your paths.

A house becomes part of us, familiar, taken for
    granted
until the time comes for change
and we see it as a blessing, a refuge,
an anchor holding firmly against the unknown.

New places will become old places,
filled with the same comfort and security
if we come to them in faith.

Strangers will become old friends
if we open our hearts and our doors.

Jesus often wandered without a settled home,
less rooted than foxes and nesting birds,
and he called others to follow him in the way:
but he told them of his Father's house,
a place prepared for them.

Live thankful for a place that is home;
live so that the eternal home shall become
    familiar,
because it is more full of love than we can
    comprehend.

*

The Lord will keep your going out and your
coming in from this time forth and for evermore.

Before a Journey

Travel is not such a rare or difficult matter as it used to be. Many of us travel daily, all at some time in our lives. When journeys were infrequent and often perilous, it was customary in religious communities and elsewhere to offer prayers for a good journey and a safe return. Although travelling is generally much safer today, it is natural to pray for one about to travel, and to commit the journey into the hands of God. There may still be a sense of adventure and opportunity in travelling, with the excitement of discovering new people and places. There are many journeys in the Bible, often begun at the command of God. Let them be our pattern of obedience and trust when we travel, and a reminder that any journey is a small image of the whole journey of human life.

*

Then Tobit called his son and said to him, 'Son, prepare supplies for the journey and set out with your brother. May God in heaven bring you safely there and return you in good health to me; and may his angel, my son, accompany you both on your journey. But his mother began to weep, and said to Tobit, 'Why is it that your have sent my child away? Is he not the staff of our hand as he goes in and out before us?' Tobit said to her, 'Do not worry; our child will leave in good health and return to us in good health. Your eyes will see him on the day when he returns to you in good health. Say no more! Do not fear for them, my sister. For a good angel will accompany him; his journey will be successful, and he will come back in good health.'

Tobit 5:17–18, 21–2

When our days there were ended, we left and proceeded on our journey; and all of them, with wives and children, escorted us outside the city. There we knelt down on the beach and prayed and said farewell to one another. Then we went on board the ship, and they returned home.

Acts 21:5–6

Before a Journey

Alone with none but Thee, my God,
   I journey on my way;
What need I fear, when Thou art near,
   O King of night and day?
More safe I am within Thy hand
Than if a host did round me stand.

St Columba

Men were created to move, as birds to fly; what they learn by nature, that reason joined to nature teacheth us. In one word I will say what can be said upon this subject; every soil is to a valiant man his own country, as the sea to the fishes. We are citizens of the whole world, yea, not of this world, but of that to come. All our life is a pilgrimage. God for his only begotten Son's sake (the true Mercury of travellers) bring us that are here strangers safely into our true country.

Fynes Moryson

*

God our Father, in your mercy be with the one who is about to travel. Grant a safe journey, fulfilment of purpose and a happy return. Be with all who love the traveller, give them confidence in your care, and patience to wait serenely until all are brought together again.

Loving God, as we pray for this one journey, we pray also for all those who travel and for those who make their journeys possible. Open the eyes that see new sights, to find in them the signs of your glory. Help us to know that you are always with us, that no distance sets you farther away, for you live in us and we in you.

Favourably receive, O Lord, our supplication for thy servant who is about to go on a journey, and for whom we pour forth our prayer; entreating thy Majesty that thou wilt send for him/her the angel of thy goodness, who may return him/her safely home.

Gallican Sacramentary (adapted)

V   May God in heaven bring you safely there
R   And guide your feet into the way of peace.
V   The Lord will go before you
R   And the God of Israel will be your rearguard.
V   God shall give his angels charge over you
R   To keep you in all your ways.
V   The Lord watch between you and me
R   When we are absent from each other.

As I go on my way, hold me in your care
safe from harm and free from sin.

Before a Journey

I shall meet many people for a short time,
and some may make me feel impatient,
and some will find me irritating –
Lord, help me to travel with love and
consideration.

Please be my guide in new places,
my light when the way forward seems
uncertain.

Bless my home and those I love,
watch between us while we are apart,
and bring me back when journeying is done.

Jesus travelled many miles, often weary and in
danger,
always healing, teaching, pardoning people as he
passed by.

Lord, make this journey part of my pilgrimage
to you;
as I go on my way, cleanse me and make me
whole.

*

Let us go forth in peace, in the name of Christ.

Retirement

The end of regular paid work is inevitably a time of some anxiety as the familiar pattern of life suddenly changes. However, it has many compensations, for people tend to live longer than in the past, and there are many more opportunities both for service and for pleasure. Most people enjoy their retirement once the adjustment has been made. As at all times of change, we should open both our anxiety and our expectations before God, offering to him the new opportunities that come with greater leisure. Life continues to develop, and there is time for more study and reflection about our faith. Time for prayer, including intercession for others, will continue and increase even when other activities become more restricted. Jesus said that he came so that we might have life more abundantly, and his promise does not fail as the years pass. This is an occasion to mark with hope and praise.

★

Retirement

Even to your old age I am he, even when you turn
grey I will carry you. I have made, and I will bear;
I will carry and will save. Remember the former
things of old; for I am God, and there is no other;
I am God and there is no one like me, declaring
the end from the beginning and from ancient
times things not yet done, saying, 'My purpose
shall stand, and I will fulfil my intention'.

Isaiah 46:4, 9–10

O God, from my youth you have taught me, and
I still proclaim your wondrous deeds. So even to
old age and grey hairs, O God, do not forsake me,
until I proclaim your might to all the generations
to come.

Psalm 71:17–18·

Master, now you are dismissing your servant in
peace, according to your word; for my eyes have
seen your salvation, which you have prepared in
the presence of all peoples, a light for revelation
to the Gentiles and for glory to your people Israel.

Luke 2:29–32

Grow old along with me!
The best is yet to be,
The last of life, for which the first was made:
Our times are in His hand
Who saith 'A whole I planned,
Youth shows but half; trust God: see all nor be
afraid!'
So, take and use Thy work:
Amend what flaws may lurk,
What strain of the stuff, what warpings past the
aim!
My times be in Thy hand!
Perfect the cup as planned!
Let age approve of youth, and death complete
the same!

Robert Browning

Having passed over this day, Lord, I give thanks
unto thee.
The evening draweth nigh, make it comfortable.
As evening there is, as of the day, so of this life.
Tarry thou with me, Lord, for it is toward
evening with me,
and the day is far spent of this my toilsome life.
Let thy strength be made perfect in my
weakness.

Lancelot Andrewes

Retirement

Thy thoughts and feelings shall not die
Nor leave thee when grey hairs are nigh,
A melancholy slave;
But an old age serene and bright
And lovely as a Lapland night
Shall lead thee to thy grave.

William Wordsworth

★

Loving Father, bless the years ahead with the love that has been unfailing in the years that have passed. Grant health of mind and body, light to discern new ways of your guiding and the grace to follow them. May all that remains of life be a faithful journey in this world towards eternal life in your presence.

Almighty God, bless all those whose lives are touched by this time of change: family and friends, former workers together, and the one who will take up the work that is left. Grant that many shall be enriched by the experience and wisdom that now finds new opportunities in your service.

V So teach us to number our years
R **That we may apply our hearts unto wisdom.**
V The righteous flourish like the palm tree,
R **In old age they still produce fruit.**
V Surely goodness and mercy shall follow me
R **All the days of my life.**

73

V I came that they might have life
R **And might have it more abundantly.**

It is hard to let go, to relax the grasp on any
    part of life:
but there is no life without change,
without leaving the old and greeting the new
until we move at last from one life to another.

We are all afraid of no longer being useful,
of having nothing more to contribute:
but we can be sure that what is most useful
is not only in the bustle of activity and
    immediate results.

Some of the best things in God's world have been
    done by people with time to sit and think,
time to reach out and find him in the stillness.

He is always there, close to us, within us,
and all people equally precious in his sight:
but there is a special blessing for those who
    know how to be quiet,
just to sit and let him love them.

Simeon found light at the end
and surrendered his past into God's future.

*

Jesus said, 'I am with you always, even to the
end of the world.'

Illness

Life cannot be enjoyed to the full without physical health. It is natural that the sick should always have a place in prayers of intercession, both private and corporate. Modern medicine has greatly improved the chance of recovery and the successful treatment of cases which not very long ago would have been incurable, but illness remains a reality in our human condition. At one time there was too much emphasis on illness being God's judgement for sin. Nevertheless, while we accept the fact that ill health can have many different causes, we do well to remember that body, mind and spirit are intimately connected and not to neglect the possible complexity of any condition. Jesus sometimes pronounced forgiveness of sins before effecting a physical cure. His work of healing was a continual feature of his earthly ministry and the power was transmitted to the Apostles. Spiritual healing is well attested today as in the past and the wisest treatment will draw on both medical and spiritual skills. We rightly pray for healing, for strength and courage in adversity, and for the insights which affliction may bring.

*

My child, when you are ill, do not delay,
  but pray to the Lord, and he will heal you.
Give up your faults and direct your hands
    rightly,
  and cleanse your heart from all sin.
Then give the physician his place, for the Lord
    created him;
  do not let him leave you, for you need him.
There may come a time when recovery lies in
    the hands of physicians,
  for they too pray to the Lord
that he will grant them success in diagnosis
  and in healing, for the sake of preserving life.

Ecclesiasticus 38:9–10, 12–14

Jesus went throughout Galilee, teaching in their synagogues and proclaiming the good news of the kingdom and curing every disease and every sickness among the people. So his fame spread throughout all Syria, and they brought to him all the sick, those who were afflicted with various diseases and pains, demoniacs, epileptics, and paralytics, and he cured them.

Matthew 4:23–4

Illness

Are any among you sick? They should call for the elders of the church and have them pray over them, anointing them with oil in the name of the Lord. The prayer of faith will save the sick, and the Lord will raise them up, and anyone who has committed sins will be forgiven.

James 5:14–15

God often permits that we should suffer a little to purify our souls, and oblige us to continue with Him. Take courage, offer Him your pains incessantly, pray to Him for strength to endure them. Above all, get a habit of entertaining yourself often with God, and forget Him the least you can. Adore Him in your infirmities, offer yourself to Him from time to time; and, in the height of your sufferings, beseech Him humbly and affectionately (as a child his father) to make you conformable to His holy will.

Brother Lawrence

I myself have felt, when ill, a sense of dependence on God, and nearness to Him, which I have seldom realised so powerfully when in health. I have also in such circumstances, when all worldly and ordinary occupations were felt to be impossible, had a relish for reading the Bible, and a profit in perusing it, such as I have experienced at no other times. I might refer to other things, but I only wish to illustrate that to get good out of sorrow is the great matter, without affirming that we are getting all the good and the intended good from it.

George Wilson

*

Merciful God, be near to the one who is troubled with sickness; in the power of your love, bring relief from present suffering and the return of health; that being made whole in body, mind and spirit, he/she may give thanks again in the fellowship of the Church and follow your will to the end of life in this world.

Be with all who work for healing, especially those who now minister to this sick person with professional skill or with loving care. Bless them with patience and compassion in their work and grant that in due time they will share in thanks for health restored.

O God of heavenly strength, who dost drive out all weakness and disease from human nature by the power of thy precepts, be favourable to thy servant *N*, that his/her infirmities may be put to flight and his/her strength established, and with

health restored he/she may straightway bless thy
holy name.

Gelasian Sacramentary

V Do not forsake me, O Lord:
R O my God, do not be far from me.
V Make haste to help me,
R O Lord, my salvation.
V Relieve the troubles of my heart,
R And bring me out of my distress.
V Consider my affliction and my trouble,
R And forgive all my sins.

The body is frail, sometimes a joy, sometimes a
    burden:
when it fails, God has not forsaken us,
for he loves the sick and his will is for their
    health.

Jesus healed the sick whenever they came to
    him
and he is still close to us, though we do not see
    him,
beside the bed of pain and weakness.

It never seems to help
when they tell us others have suffered and are
    suffering:
it is our distress, not theirs, that is real to us.

79

But Jesus suffered for us all,
the just for the unjust,
suffered in a body like ours for joy and sorrow,
revealing that out of suffering comes life and
    joy.

Nothing separates us from God:
whatever the issue, we are his much loved
    children –
not with a human father's love, however deep,
but with divine love that has known and
    accepted the human body.

*

I waited patiently for the Lord; he inclined to me
and heard my cry.

Sick Child

When a loved child is ill or hurt, members of the family feel the pain as if it were their own. The sense of helplessness, of being unable to give the comfort that has healed the previous troubles of a little life, is very hard to bear. At such a time Christians as much as anyone may feel bewilderment and even anger at the sight of innocent suffering. Yet they will try to hold fast to their trust in a loving God, knowing that we may find him closest to us in our times of distress. At the heart of the Gospel, we see human agony accepted by the incarnate God, Jesus who loved children and healed many who were sick. As we fix our eyes on the Cross, our prayers of intercession become more earnest and assured, while we offer ourselves to be used in the divine purpose and unite our care with the eternal love of the Father.

*

Out of the depths I cry to you, O Lord.
  Lord, hear my voice!
Let your ears be attentive
  to the voice of my supplications!

I wait for the Lord, my soul waits,
  and in his word I hope;
my soul waits for the Lord
  more than those who watch for the morning.

Psalm 130:1, 5–6

There was a royal official whose son lay ill in Capernaum. When he heard that Jesus had come from Judaea to Galilee, he went and begged him to come down and heal his son, for he was at the point of death. Then Jesus said to him, 'Unless you see signs and wonders you will not believe.' The official said to him, 'Sir, come down before my little boy dies.' Jesus said to him, 'Go; your son will live.' The man believed the word that Jesus spoke to him and started on his way. As he was going down, his slaves met him and told him that his child was alive. So he asked them the hour when he began to recover, and they said to him, 'Yesterday at one in the afternoon the fever left him.' The father realized that this was the hour when Jesus had said to him, 'Your son will live.' So he himself believed, along with his whole household.

John 4:46–53

82

Sick Child

Father, to thee we look in all our sorrow;
Thou art the fountain whence our healing flows;
Dark though the night, joy cometh with the
    morrow;
Safely they rest who on thy love repose.

F. L. Hosmer

Let us be thankful that our sorrow lives in us as
an indestructible force, only changing in form, as
forces do, and passing from pain to sympathy.

George Eliot

Can a mother sit and hear
An infant groan, an infant fear?
No, no! never can it be!
Never, never can it be!

And can he who smiles on all
Hear the wren with sorrows small,
Hear the small bird's grief and care,
Hear the woes that infants bear,

And not sit beside their nest,
Pouring pity in their breast;
And not sit the cradle near,
Weeping tear on infant's tear?

William Blake

★

O God, Loving Father, look with compassion on the distress of this little one. Let the strength of the Lord Jesus, who loved children and healed the sick, be with him/her at this time. Grant relief from suffering, and restored health to enjoy again all the delights of a young life growing up in your care.

Comfort, dear Lord, those who share this suffering and wait anxiously for healing. Calm their troubled minds, mercifully supply what is lacking in faith and courage, use them in your service as may be best for this child. Guide and enable doctors and nurses here and everywhere who work with sick children.

V   As a father has compassion for his children,
R   **So the Lord has compassion for those who fear him.**
V   I will restore health to you:
R   **I will heal you of your wounds, says the Lord.**
V   He heals the broken in heart
R   **And binds up their wounds.**
V   Remember your tender mercies, O Lord,
R   **For they have been from of old.**

If health and strength could be parcelled like a
   birthday gift,
what would we not give to relieve this little
   one?

Sick Child

Saints have shared pain, suffered for others,
known even strange marks of the Passion,
but here it seems we can only stand and watch,
giving what love and comfort we can.

If the pain of the world seems to be drawn into
    this little body
because love is an infinite magnifier of joy and
    sorrow,
pray that there may be a growth of compassion,
reaching from this centre to all suffering
    children in the world.

The Father who saw the agony of the Son
is not a remote God who does not care for his
    little ones:
trust in him –
for even on Calvary, the meaning was love.

★

It is not the will of your Father in heaven that one
of these little ones should perish.

Chronic or Terminal Illness

People today have a greater life-expectancy, and medical science can often prolong life in cases that would once have been fatal at an earlier stage. This has brought many blessings, but also some hard decisions and sometimes the continuation of life that has been deprived of some of its quality. A long illness may severely test the faith of sufferers and those close to them, but it can also bring new strength in learning deeper dependence on God. When we are uncertain what to ask for someone, we recognize that the best intercession is the prayer which offers that person to God's loving will. We do not like to think about death, which has become almost a forbidden topic in our time. To recognize when it may be near is not to be morbid or to hasten it, but to accept the inevitable transition from this life to the next. We must be tactful but also realistic, finding the presence of God in the situation of the moment.

*

Chronic or Terminal Illness

For everything there is a season, and a time for every matter under heaven:

a time to be born, and a time to die;
a time to plant, and a time to pluck up what is planted;
a time to kill, and a time to heal;
a time to break down, and a time to build up;
a time to weep, and a time to laugh;
a time to mourn, and a time to dance;
a time to throw away stones, and a time to gather stones together;
a time to embrace, and a time to refrain from embracing;
a time to seek, and a time to lose;
a time to keep, and a time to throw away.

Ecclesiastes 3:1–6

I consider that the sufferings of this present time are not worth comparing with the glory about to be revealed to us. For in hope we were saved. Now hope that is seen is not hope. For who hopes for what is seen? But if we hope for what we do not see, we wait for it with patience. Likewise the Spirit helps us in our weakness; for we do not know how to pray as we ought, but that very Spirit intercedes with sighs too deep for words.

Romans 8:18, 24–6

A Pastoral Prayer Book

The soul's dark cottage, battered and decayed,
Lets in new light through chinks that Time
   hath made:
Stronger by weakness, wiser men become
As they draw near to their eternal home.
Leaving the old, both worlds at once they view
That stand upon the threshold of the new.

Edmund Waller

Do not be afraid of death even though you feel it
to be imminent and have every reason for despair,
but give yourself up all the more to the mercy of
God. No one, not even the Saints, can do anything
else. They can only confide themselves hopefully
to God. Death is frightening only when it is far
off, and it is useless to think of it from our present
standpoint. I have seen many people die, and not
one of them had the slightest fear of death when
it was there.

Abbé de Tourville

My God, I know thy powerful word did frame
Out of pure nothing all that hath a name,
From the bright Angels baiting in full streams
Of deathless joys to motes that dance in beams.
And shall I doubt but such a word can call
Flesh out of dust that out of less made all?

Nathaniel Wanley

Chronic or Terminal Illness

*

Father, we do not know how to pray as we ought. Accept our prayer as we commit this sick person to your mercy, knowing that all things are yours in life and in death, and that your love never fails. Help us to find our duty and our joy in your will and keep us firm in the faith that has sustained us until this hour.

In this time of trouble, gracious Lord, we desire to give thanks for all the happiness that has been and for the love which holds us close to one another, and ask that we may face with confidence all that is to be. As we are bold to offer this suffering to be united with the pain of our Lord Jesus Christ on the Cross, we pray at last to be united with him in his Resurrection.

We beseech thee, most merciful God and Father, that as thou givest thy servants lengthened suffering, so thou wilt give them faith and patience in the acceptance of thy will, to offer themselves up without reserve to thee; that they may be purged from all the remains of their natural self, and may be accepted of thee.

Sursum Corda

V   So teach us to number our days
R   That we may apply our hearts unto wisdom.
V   It is good that people should hope
**R   And quietly wait for the salvation of the
      Lord.**
V   The Lord is my portion, says my soul,
R   Therefore I will hope in him.
V   Let not your heart be troubled
R   Neither let it be afraid.

May the spirit grow stronger as the body
    weakens,
the presence of God more real as the power of
    human help lessens.

Patience must grow from a negative bearing of
    trouble
into a greater affirmation of faith that all will be
    well,
and knowledge that God is here when nothing
    seems to change,
working through the darkness as well as the
    light.

Live in faith, without guilt when there is doubt,
live in hope, without denying reality,
live in love, finding time to pray for others who
    suffer.

Chronic or Terminal Illness

Nothing takes away what has been good and
    loving,
our pledge that the love of God is greater than
    our own:
for he loved our race against the odds, even to
    death,
and he is close to us if we trust and never let
    go.

*

Be of good courage and he will strengthen your
heart, all you who hope in the Lord.

In Bereavement

Death is the one certainty in every life, the one inevitable event. But every death, like every birth, is unique and brings change to many other people. We must not pretend that it is unimportant or underestimate its effects on those who remain. To mourn for a loved one is human and right: it is a mistake to refuse grief its full outlet. Yet the grief of Christians must be different from that of others who are without faith and hope. We live and die trusting in resurrection to eternal life, because Christ our Lord has won the victory over death. The New Testament and the works of the early Fathers of the Church continually proclaim the Christian hope which links the Resurrection of Christ with our own. We know that the faithful departed have been called by a merciful God, who receives them in the love that was revealed on the Cross and proclaimed in the Resurrection.

*

In Bereavement

If I ascend to heaven, you are there;
if I make my bed in the world of the dead, you
   are there.
If I say, 'Surely the darkness shall cover me,
   and the light around me become night',
even the darkness is not dark to you;
   the night is as bright as the day,
   for darkness is as light to you.

Psalm 139:8, 11–12

If for this life only we have hoped in Christ, we are of all people most to be pitied. But in fact Christ has been raised from the dead, the first fruits of those who have died. For since death came through a human being, the resurrection of the dead has also came through a human being; for as all die in Adam, so all will be made alive in Christ.

1 Corinthians 15:19–22

We do not want you to be uninformed, brothers and sisters, about those who have died, so that you may not grieve as others do who have no hope. For since we believe that Jesus died and rose from the dead, even so, through Jesus, God will bring with him those who have died. Therefore encourage one another with these words.

1 Thessalonians 4:13–15, 18

If Christ hath died His brethren well may die.
  Sing in the gate of death, lay by
    This life without a sigh:
For Christ hath died and good it is to die
  To sleep when he so lays us by,
    Then wake without a sigh.

Christina Rossetti

Why should I weep for thee, my most loving brother, who wast thus torn from me that thou mightest be the brother of all? For I have not lost but changed my intercourse with thee; before we were inseparable in the body, now we are undivided in affection; for thou remainest with me, and ever will remain. And indeed, whilst thou wast living with me, our country never tore thee from me, nor didst thou thyself ever prefer our country to me; and now thou art become surety for that other country. For I begin to be no stranger there where the better portion of myself already is.

St Ambrose

*

Loving Father, we commit to you the soul of *N*, confident in the love that has called him/her from this world into a new life. We give thanks for all the good things of the life that has ended here, for the

times of happiness that we have shared. Forgive now
his/her sins; grant him/her rest and peace, and the
unending joy of life closer to you. We put our trust
in Jesus Christ your Son our Lord, who lived and
died for our salvation and rose from death so that
we might have eternal life.

Dear God of mercy, come close to those who mourn.
Comfort them in assurance of the love that never
dies; bless them in the happy memories of the past;
give them strength in all that is to come, with trust
in the Resurrection that gives them union now and
for ever with those they have loved.

Give rest, O Christ, to your servant with your
 saints: where sorrow and pain are no more,
 neither sighing, but life everlasting.
You only are immortal, the Creator and maker
 of Man:
And we are mortal, formed of the earth, and to
 earth shall we return:
For so you did ordain when you created me,
 saying,
Dust you are, and to dust you shall return.
All we go down into the dust; and weeping at
 the grave we make our song:
Alleluia, Alleluia, Alleluia.

Russian Contakion of the Departed

May the soul of N and the souls of all the faithful
rest in peace and rise in glory.

V   Though I walk through the valley of the
     shadow of death
R   I fear no evil, for you are with me.
V   Blessed are they that die in the Lord,
R   For they rest from their labours.
V   Blessed are they that mourn
R   For they shall be comforted.
V   As in Adam all die
R   Even so in Christ shall all be made alive.

Sorrow is real, a harsh truth that twists us with
     pain,
a burden that bends us down to breaking:
but it is not a burden that we bear alone.

Christ, lifted up to the death of the Cross,
lifts us with him and shows us the way ahead.

We worship before the Cross, which is joy out
     of sorrow,
life out of death, the signpost to heaven.

The Christian soul passes from the temporary to
     the eternal,
from this small world to the infinite,
from the company of a few to the company of
     all the faithful.

In Bereavement

Where we see only loss and emptiness,
God sees new life, a vacant place filled.

Nothing that has been good and lovely can ever
  perish:
we must go on living as long as it is required,
strengthened by the past, patiently confident for
  the future.

★

Jesus said, 'I am the Resurrection and the Life: he
who believes in me, though he were dead, yet shall
he live'.

Death of a Child

There are few sorrows in this world greater than grief for a dead child. Many parents have suffered this deep distress at the sudden ending of a new life that seemed full of promise. In the Bible there are several stories of such losses, and death in childhood continued to be sadly frequent for many centuries that followed. Today, when infant mortality is lower, the pain is perhaps even harder to bear than in the past. It may be some comfort to know that the very young, like the very old, seem to slip away from life easily and are usually spared a slow decline. But at such a time, there is little that can mitigate grief. Christians can only cling to the cross which is the emblem of pain borne by divine manhood, and try to believe in the loving purpose of God which seems hidden. If all things, even the deepest sorrow, can be offered to God, the lives that must go on will be richer in faith. It is a hard saying, but many have proved its truth.

★

Death of a Child

David said, 'While the child was still alive, I fasted and wept; for I said, "Who knows? The Lord may be gracious to me, and the child may live." But now he is dead; why should I fast? Can I bring him back again? I shall go to him, but he will not return to me.'

2 Samuel 12:22–3

The Lord will not reject for ever. Although he causes grief, he will have compassion according to the abundance of his steadfast love; for he does not willingly afflict or grieve anyone.

Lamentations 3:31–3

They will hunger no more, and thirst no more; the sun will not strike them, nor any scorching heat; for the Lamb at the centre of the throne will be their shepherd, and he will guide them to springs of the water of life, and God will wipe away every tear from their eyes.

Revelation 7:16–17

We give him/her back to thee, O God, who gave him/her to us. Yet as thou didst not lose him/her in the giving, so we do not lose him/her by his/her return. Not as the world gives, givest thou, O lover of souls. What thou givest, thou takest not away, for what is thine is ours also if we are thine.

A Pastoral Prayer Book

And life is eternal and love is eternal, and death is a horizon, and a horizon is nothing save the line of our sight. Lifts us up, strong Son of God, that we may see further; cleanse our eyes that we may know ourselves to be nearer to our loved ones who are with thee. And while thou dost prepare a place for us, prepare us also for that happy place, that where thou art we may be also for evermore.

William Penn

Farewell dear babe, my heart's too much
    content,
Farewell sweet babe, the pleasure of mine eye,
Farewell fair flower, that for a space was lent,
Then ta'en away unto Eternity.
Blest babe, why should I once bewail thy fate,
Or sigh thy days so soon were terminate,
Since thou art settled in an everlasting state?

By nature trees do rot when they are grown,
And plums and apples thorough ripe do fall,
And corn and grass are in their season mown,
And time brings down what is both strong and
    tall.
But plants now set to be eradicate,
And buds new blown to have so short a date,
Is by His hand alone that guides nature and fate.

Anne Bradstreet

Death of a Child

Death came unheralded: but it was well;
For so thy Saviour bore
Kind witness, thou wast meet at once to dwell
   On His eternal shore;
      All warning spared
For none He gives where hearts are for prompt
   change prepared.

Joy of sad hearts, and light of downcast eyes!
   Dearest, thou art enshrined
In all thy fragrance in our memories;
      For we must ever find
         Bare thought, of thee
Freshen this weary life, while weary life shall
   be.

John Henry Newman

*

Almighty God, we pray for these parents in their
distress and trouble: comfort them with your presence, with the confidence of your love that never
fails even in the times of darkness. May they grow
closer together in love as they share their grief and
strengthen each other in the days and years ahead.
Enfold them in the love of family and friends, and
restore them to the joy of life.

Loving God, we commit into your hands the soul of this little one who has been called away from this world. We know that nothing is made in vain: grant that what there was of life shall find its meaning in your loving purpose. Draw us closer together in remembering him/her and unite us in the power of the Resurrection, in which we are for ever one.

O Lord, you have made us very small, and we bring our years to an end like a tale that is told; help us to remember that beyond our brief day is the eternity of your love.

Reinhold Niebuhr

V I cry to you, O Lord, give heed to my cry,
R For I am brought very low.
V As a father has compassion for his children,
R So the Lord has compassion for those who fear him.
V He knows how we are made,
R He remembers we are dust.
V The Lord gives and the Lord has taken away:
R He gives sleep to his beloved.

We stand in a dark place
for the light of a little life has gone out
and there seems no way to turn in confidence.

Death of a Child

Dreams of what might have been torment us
but we do not know if the years would have
  brought great trouble,
what pain to come is cancelled in the pain of
  this time:
one day perhaps all will be made clear.

Now there is nothing but to pour our sorrow
into the well of sorrow that God watches in
  love
and turns into living water.

Surely he knows a father's pain
and Mary watched her child, grown to
  manhood, dying in agony:
she stood by the Cross,
and after the Cross there is Resurrection.

May this cross we bear be the way to new life,
strength to go on believing and serving,
strength to go on living while life is granted,
to value each day of life, because now we know
that life is very precious, very fragile,
that life and death are in the hands of God.

*

Jesus said, 'In heaven their angels do always
behold the face of my Father, who is in heaven'.

Anniversary of Death

Influenced as we are by the rhythms of the year, it is a natural human instinct to make a yearly remembrance on the anniversary of the death of one known and loved. The Church commemorated the faithful departed in the earliest services which have come down to us, and there was especial celebration of those who had died for their faith. The feasts of martyrs and other saints are still widely observed in our public worship. Many Christians like to remember in prayer the departed who have no public memorial but are still close to the hearts of the living. As the years pass, sorrow finds some relief and the happy memories of a past life predominate. We want to give thanks that the loved one is free from pain and suffering, secure in the hand of God, and that we shall in time be reunited. As we think of the individual, we are drawn closer into the fellowship of the whole Church, living here on earth and living also in the fuller life of eternity.

★

Anniversary of Death

The souls of the righteous are in the hand of God, and no torment will ever touch them. In the eyes of the foolish they seemed to have died, and their departure was thought to be a disaster, and their going from us to be their destruction; but they are at peace. For though in the sight of others they were punished, their hope is full of immortality.

Wisdom of Solomon 3:1–4

You have come to Mount Zion and to the city of the living God, the heavenly Jerusalem, and to innumerable angels in festive gathering, and to the assembly of the firstborn who are enrolled in heaven, and to God the judge of all, and to the spirits of the righteous made perfect, and to Jesus, the mediator of a new covenant, and to the sprinkled blood that speaks a better word than the blood of Abel.

Hebrews 12:22–4

I heard a voice from heaven saying, 'Write this: Blessed are the dead who from now on die in the Lord.' 'Yes,' says the Spirit, 'they will rest from their labours, for their deeds follow them.'

Revelation 14:13

A Pastoral Prayer Book

They are all gone into the world of light,
   And I alone sit lingering here;
Their very memory is fair and bright,
   And my sad thoughts doth clear.

I see them walking in an air of glory,
   Whose light doth trample on my days:
My days which are but dull and hoary,
   Mere glimmerings and decays.

O holy hopes, and high humility!
   High as the heavens above!
Those are your walks, and you have showed
   them me
     To kindle my cold love.

Henry Vaughan

Yonder there is no end of singing, yonder there is
no end of praise, yonder there is no end of remembering every past trouble; never will it cease, the
praise of God in our Father's house. A beginning
of song, a beginning of praise – such, O Jesus, at
the end of a thousand long ages, will be the joy of
the pilgrims yonder at the end of their road; there
will never be an end to the sound of the golden
harp.

William Williams

*

Anniversary of Death

O God, as we remember *N* who is no longer with us but is for ever with you, we give thanks for all the good and happy memories and renew our trust in your mercy that he/she, in the company of all the faithful departed, is at rest with joy and peace in your heavenly kingdom.

Grant, O Father, that we may so live our lives here that our faith in the resurrection to everlasting life may appear in all we do, and that we shall follow the paths that you have ordained for us as members of the whole Church, of the living and the dead, who are held securely in your unfailing love.

O Lord our God, from whom neither life nor death can separate those who trust in thy love, and whose love holds in its embrace thy children in this world and the next; so unite us to thy self that in fellowship with thee we may always be united to our loved ones whether here or there; give us courage, constancy and hope; through him who was buried and rose again for us, Jesus Christ our Lord.

William Temple

Let us give thanks before God for all those who rejoice with us, but upon another shore and in a greater light, that multitude which no man can

A Pastoral Prayer Book

number, whose hope was in the Word made flesh,
and with whom, in the Lord Jesus, we for evermore are one.

Christmas Bidding Prayer

V Ye spirits and souls of the righteous, bless
   ye the Lord,
R Praise him and magnify him for ever.
V They are before the throne of God
**R And serve him day and night within his
   temple.**
V They will hunger no more and thirst no
   more
**R And God will wipe away all tears from their
   eyes.**
V Whether we live, we live unto the Lord,
R And whether we die, we die unto the Lord.

Memory is a strange thing, not always to be
   commanded,
not always to be trusted when it comes:
our memory of the dead we have loved is not
   only in the mind –
it is deep within us, a part of us, never leaving
   us.

It is part of God's love in us, always constant,
making no account of time or place, life or
   death.

108

Anniversary of Death

Each year may seem long, sometimes weary,
   sometimes lonely,
unless we share it with those who are out of
   time,
united in the timelessness of God
for whom a thousand years are as yesterday.

We cannot conceive of being in the presence of
   God,
except by imperfect images of light and music,
or above all the perfect image
of God made man, made like us, gone before us,
   ever with us.

When we remember the dead with love,
we remember that we too are called to eternal
   life.

★

With the saints give rest, O Christ, to the soul of
thy servant *N*, where there is neither sickness, nor
sorrow, nor sighing, but life everlasting.

Orthodox Liturgy

In Time of Trouble

Many of the problems and sorrows of life come to us in familiar forms, known in every generation: illness, bereavement, separation and the like. Others are not so readily classified and these can perhaps make the sufferer feel more lonely and distressed than those that are easily shared and understood. Even what may seem a slight trouble to one outside the situation can be immensely distressing to those who experience it. At such times, family and close friends can be a strong support and the time of trouble often strengthens relationships from which comfort has come. As we look to the Cross which is at the heart of Christian faith, we feel the compassion of God and the triumph of goodness over evil. The darkness will lift, but as it envelops us we pray for the light of the divine presence with us.

★

In Time of Trouble

The thought of my affliction and my homeless-
ness is wormwood and gall! My soul continually
thinks of it and is bowed down within me. But
this I call to mind, and therefore I have hope: the
steadfast love of the Lord never ceases, his mercies
never come to an end; they are new every morning; great is your faithfulness. 'The Lord is my
portion,' says my soul, 'therefore I will hope in
him.' The Lord is good to those who wait for him,
to the soul that seeks him. It is good that one
should wait quietly for the salvation of the Lord.

Lamentations 3:19–26

The wilderness and the dry land shall be glad,
   the desert shall rejoice and blossom;
like the crocus it shall blossom abundantly,
   and rejoice with joy and singing.
The glory of Lebanon shall be given to it,
   the majesty of Carmel and Sharon.
They shall see the glory of the Lord,
   the majesty of our God.
Strengthen the weak hands,
   and make firm the feeble knees.
Say to those who are of a fearful heart,
   'Be strong, do not fear!'

Isaiah 35:1–4

Humble yourselves therefore under the mighty hand of God, so that he may exalt you in due time. Cast all your anxiety on him, because he cares for you. Discipline yourselves; keep alert. Like a roaring lion your adversary the devil prowls around, looking for someone to devour. Resist him, steadfast in your faith, for your brothers and sisters throughout the world are undergoing the same kinds of suffering. And after you have suffered for a little while, the God of all grace, who has called you to his eternal glory in Christ, will himself restore, support, strengthen and establish you.

1 Peter 5. 6–10

In the desolate time, when I feel perplexed and forsaken, I would think upon the cross of my Saviour and his dreadful cry, that my faith may hold fast in his faith and that despair may not seize me. Help me to remember the days of vision and sure confidence, guide me to stay my soul in the revelation of thyself which thou hast given me in time past through all thy prophets and servants, and bring me out of the valley of the dark shade once more into the light of thy presence, through Jesus Christ our Lord.

W. R. Matthews

In Time of Trouble

I shall know why, when time is over.
And I have ceased to wonder why;
Christ will explain each separate anguish
In the fair schoolroom of the sky.

He will tell me what Peter promised,
And I, for wonder at his woe,
I shall forget the drop of anguish
That scalds me now, that scalds me now.

Emily Dickinson

Most people have had a period in their lives when they have felt forsaken; when, having long hoped against hope, and still seen the day of fruition deferred, their hearts have truly sickened within them. This is a terrible hour, but it is often that darkest point which precedes the rise of day; that turn of the year when the icy January wind carries over the waste at once the dirge of departing winter, and the prophecy of coming spring. Let whoever grieves still cling fast to love and faith in God: God will never deceive, never finally desert us. 'Whom he loveth he chasteneth.' These words are true, and should not be forgotten.

Charlotte Brontë

Let nothing disturb thee.
Nothing affright thee;
All things are passing;
God never changeth.
Patient endurance attaineth to all things;
Who God possesseth in nothing is wanting:
Alone God sufficeth.

St Teresa of Avila

★

Merciful Father, look upon our trouble and enfold us in your love; Jesus, who bore our sins and sorrows, strengthen our faith; Holy Spirit, guide us in all we do until this time has passed, and keep us in the right way in all that is to come.

As we offer our anxiety, we are mindful of the many sorrows of the world. May this trial make us more open in compassion, more constant in prayer for the needs of others, more steadfast in faith and hope and love.

O God by whom the meek are guided in judgement, and light riseth up in darkness for the godly, grant us, in all our doubts and uncertainties, the grace to ask what thou wouldest have us do; that the Spirit of Wisdom may save us from all false choices and that in thy light we may see light,

In Time of Trouble

and in the straight path may not stumble; through
Jesus Christ our Lord.

William Bright

V Come to me all you who labour and are
     heavy laden,
R And I will give you rest.
V Take my yoke upon you and learn of me,
R For my yoke is easy and my burden is light.
V Wonderfully show your steadfast love,
R Hide me in the shadow of your wings.
V My help comes from the Lord,
R Who made heaven and earth.

In bad times like this
we may be told to think of others who are
    worse off,
and remember how Job was patient in suffering;
but this is not Job's trouble; it is all ours.

Because this trouble is ours, human trouble, it
    is also God's,
who took our nature and bore our sorrows.

Jesus loved those who came to him in their
    emptiness
and on the Cross he was totally emptied and
    helpless.

He said, 'Take up your cross,' and it is heavy,
but always in church there is the cross,
and before he went to the Cross he said, 'Thy
  will be done.'
It is hard for us to say it, but he said it also for
  us.

After the Cross there was life:
may we find, from this point of death, a
  resurrection.

*

The eternal God is thy refuge, and underneath are
the everlasting arms.

In Time of Rejoicing

Much of our prayer is concerned with seeking help and comfort in times of trouble. It is natural to turn to God, our loving Father, when things go wrong: do we turn so readily when we are happy? We are more inclined to ask than to give thanks, but worship that does not celebrate the joy of life is incomplete. A truly grateful heart is an acceptable offering, but we sometimes need words to focus our gratitude and help our understanding. As trouble which seems slight to others may be heavy for those who bear it, so unspectacular occasions of joy may be deeply meaningful. Like the woman in the parable who found the lost coin and called her neighbours to rejoice with her, we want to share our happiness with others who will join in our time of praise. God made all things well, and a world damaged by sin is still a world in which his gifts are abundant.

*

A Pastoral Prayer Book

O give thanks to the Lord, call on his name,
  make known his deeds among the peoples.
Sing to him, sing praises to him;
  tell of all his wonderful works.
Glory in his holy name;
  let the hearts of those who seek the Lord
  rejoice;
Seek the Lord and his strength;
  seek his presence continually.
Remember the wonderful works he has done,
  his miracles, and the judgements he has
  uttered.

Psalm 105:1–5

Be filled with the Spirit, as you sing psalms and hymns and spiritual songs among yourselves, singing and making melody to the Lord in your hearts, giving thanks to God the Father at all times and for everything in the name of our Lord Jesus Christ.

Ephesians 5:18–20

Your enjoyment of the world is never right, till you so esteem it, that everything in it is more your treasure than a king's exchequer full of gold and silver. And that exchequer yours also in its place and service. Can you take too much joy in your Father's works?

Thomas Traherne

In Time of Rejoicing

Thou that hast given so much to me,
Give one thing more, a grateful heart.
See how thy beggar works on thee
      By art.

Not thankful when it pleaseth me;
As if they blessings had spare days:
But such a heart, whose pulse may be
      Thy praise.

George Herbert

It is probable that in most of us the spiritual life is impoverished and stunted because we give so little place to gratitude. It is more important to thank God for blessings received than to pray for them beforehand. For that forward-looking prayer, though right as an expression of dependence upon God, is still self-centred, in part at least, of its interest; there is something we hope to gain by our prayer. But the backward-looking act of thanksgiving is quite free from this. In itself it is quite selfless. Thus it is akin to love. All our love to God is in response to his love for us; it never starts on our side.

William Temple

A Pastoral Prayer Book

O Lord, that lends me life,
Lend me a heart replete with thankfulness.

William Shakespeare

★

Most loving Father, accept our thanks for all the good things we receive from you, and especially for this present time of happiness. As we share our joy with others, help us always to be ready to rejoice with those who rejoice as well as to comfort those who are sad. We know that you care for us in the little things as well as in the great and that all is held firmly in your love.

May this present joy, gracious Lord, be for us a token of the great, immeasurable love with which you have sustained us in our lives and enriched us with the gift of faith and above all with knowledge of the redemption by which we are united with you both now and in the life to come.

V Praise the Lord, O my soul,
R **And all that is within me, bless his holy Name.**
V Give thanks to the Lord, for he is good,
R **And his mercy endures for ever.**
V In everything give thanks,
R **For this is the will of God in Jesus Christ.**

In Time of Rejoicing

V   I will give thanks to the Lord with my
       whole heart,
R   I will tell of all your wonderful deeds.

It is such a little thing to say 'Thank you':
often the unthought words of a passing
    moment.

To say it to God, Creator, Sustainer, Redeemer,
is a more serious thing;
to know that we can dare to say it,
and that our words are accepted,
is a thing most wonderful and never to be
    forgotten.

In the beginning God saw everything that he
    had made
and it was very good;
and the little things that we count as happiness
are for ever part of the eternal love that blessed
    creation.

Let us make our 'Thank you' a return of love
    for love,
a response that is not selfish or calculated
but answers a divine love that paid the price of
    loving.

And let us live as if we mean what we say.

★

Rejoice evermore. Pray without ceasing. In everything give thanks.